Gerald R. Ford

Gerald R. Ford

R. Conrad Stein

AMERICA'S
38TH
PRESIDENT

Children's Press®
A Division of Scholastic Inc.
New York / Toronto / London / Auckland / Sydney
Mexico City / New Delhi / Hong Kong
Danbury, Connecticut

Library of Congress Cataloging-in-Publication Data

Stein, R. Conrad.
      Gerald R. Ford / R. Conrad Stein.
         p. cm. — (Encyclopedia of presidents)
Includes bibliographical references and index.
  ISBN 0-516-22973-7
  1. Ford, Gerald R., 1913– —Juvenile literature. 2. Presidents—United
States—Biography—Juvenile literature. I. Title. II. Series.
E866.S74 2005
973.925'092—dc22   2004017773

Contents

Chapter 1

A Leader in Troubled Times —————

"My fellow Americans, our long national nightmare is over. Our Constitution works. Our great Republic is a government of laws and not of men. Here the people rule." Gerald R. Ford spoke these words on August 9, 1974, the day he became the 38th president of the United States.

Ford took office in troubled times. He became president when President Richard M. Nixon resigned from office in disgrace after a scandal that rocked the nation's trust in its government. The United States was also recovering from the long and divisive war in Vietnam. Inflation and high unemployment were causing difficulties for businesses and working people.

Gerald Ford led the nation in a calm, reassuring manner, helping to restore faith in government and ease political conflict. People

Gerald Ford is sworn in as president by Chief Justice Warren Burger on August 9, 1974, hours after President Nixon resigned. Ford's wife Betty is at center.

trusted him. He was seen as a practical man who grew up in a working-class family, one who would not lie to his fellow Americans. In his youth, Ford was a star football player. He once said, "Thanks to my football experience, I know the value of team play. I believe it is one of the most important lessons to be learned and practiced in our lives."

Ford served as president for just two and a half years. Some historians have called him an "accidental president." He became vice president on December 6, 1973, without being elected. Eight months later he assumed the office of president after Nixon's resignation. He was the first person in history to serve as vice president and president without gaining election to either office. Ford ran for a full term in 1976, but lost in a close election. He then retired and returned to private life. During his retirement he wrote his autobiography, in which he described the deep wounds that scarred the country when he took office in 1974 and the actions he took to ease the nation's pain. Appropriately, the book was called *A Time to Heal*.

Boyhood

The future president was born in Omaha, Nebraska, on July 14, 1913. The circumstances of his early life were troubling. His parents were Omaha businessman Leslie King and his wife Dorothy King. He was named Leslie Lynch King after his father. Despite having a healthy, blond baby boy, Leslie and Dorothy King were unhappy and they argued constantly. Leslie King, who had a violent temper, sometimes hit his wife.

Through much of American history divorce was considered shameful, and many couples lived for decades in unhappy marriages. Gerald Ford was the first president who was the child of divorced parents.

☆ ☆ ☆

In December 1913, Dorothy King separated from her husband and moved back to Grand Rapids, Michigan, where her parents lived. The next year, a court in Omaha granted Dorothy a divorce from Leslie King, finding him "guilty of extreme cruelty." Dorothy hoped to build a new life for herself and her son in Grand Rapids.

In 1914 Grand Rapids was Michigan's second-largest city, with nearly 150,000 people. It was most famous for its furniture factories, which produced millions of desks for offices and schools. It was also known as a religious city, served by more than 130 churches. Many of its

Dorothy King and her young son Leslie King in early 1914. Mrs. King later married Gerald Ford Sr., and Leslie was named Gerald Ford after his adoptive father.

residents were immigrants or children of immigrants who had arrived from the Netherlands in the late 1800s.

Dorothy met Gerald Rudolf Ford at a church social. He was a big man who almost shook the walls with his roaring laughs. Ford worked as a paint salesman. He soon came to love Dorothy and her young son. In February 1916, Gerald and Dorothy were married. Dorothy's son was renamed Gerald Ford to honor his new father. (As a young adult, he changed his name legally to Gerald Rudolph Ford.)

In the next few years, the Ford family grew and prospered. They welcomed three more sons, Thomas (born 1918), Richard (born 1924), and James (born 1927). During the 1920s, a mood of confidence prevailed in the country. Gerald Ford Sr. worked hard to become the top paint salesman at the Grand Rapids Wood Finishing Company. Still, the family was subject to sudden financial reversals. Ford later wrote, "Neither of my parents could be described as 'secure' economically; but emotionally both were very secure."

Jerry Ford was good most of the time, but he had a quick temper and sometimes threw ugly tantrums. Jerry's mother was determined to control the tantrums before they got worse. She would send Jerry to his bedroom and not let him come out until he had calmed down. Once, after a display of anger, she gave Jerry the poem "If," by Rudyard Kipling. "Read this and profit from it," she

Jerry Ford (left) with a cousin after a day of fishing.

insisted. "It'll help you control that temper of yours." Her discipline was always

motivated by love. In time Jerry learned to curb his moods.

Even in the second and third grades the future president excelled in sports.

His school had only a gravel playground, but the boys still played tackle football.

" I f "

The poem "If" by Rudyard Kipling begins with these lines:

> If you can keep your head when all about you
>
> Are losing theirs and blaming it on you,
>
> If you can trust yourself when all men doubt you
>
> But make allowance for their doubting too,
>
> If you can wait and not be tired by waiting,
>
> Or being lied about, don't deal in lies,
>
> Or being hated, don't give way to hating,
>
> And yet don't look too good, nor talk too wise:

It ends:

> If you can fill the unforgiving minute
>
> With sixty seconds' worth of distance run,
>
> Yours is the Earth and everything that's in it,
>
> And—which is more—you'll be a Man, my son!

☆ ☆ ☆

Jerry regularly came home with bruised elbows and scratched knees. He also formed a secret club. Near the Ford home stood an old two-story garage. Jerry and a few of his chums would sneak into the garage, climb a ladder to the loft, and play poker for pennies. "It was a great hideaway," he wrote, "because my parents wouldn't climb the ladder to get to the second floor—or so I thought. My stepfather, however, knew better. He caught us red-handed several times and reprimanded us severely."

Jerry Ford was left-handed. This posed a problem in those days because teachers often forced left-handers to write with their right hands. Trying to change may have brought on a problem with stuttering. "Some words gave me fits, and it would take me forever to get them out," he later wrote. The stutter disappeared by the time he was ten, and he continued to write with his left hand. Oddly, Ford threw a football or baseball with his *right* hand. "For as long as I can remember," he explained, "I have been left-handed when I'm sitting down and right-handed standing up."

At an early age Jerry joined the Boy Scouts, in which his father was an active volunteer. The scoutmaster at Troop 15 described Jerry as "a born leader." Jerry advanced through the ranks, reaching Eagle Scout, the highest level in scouting. For the rest of his life he kept his Eagle Scout badge, calling it a "treasured possession."

The Ford home at 649 Union Street SE, in Grand Rapids.

A Visit From a Stranger ——————————

When Jerry was 12 or 13, his mother told him for the first time that Gerald Ford
Sr. was not his real father. No doubt this news came as a shock, but Jerry loved his
father and Gerald Ford Sr. returned that love.

Jerry Ford at 14 (second from left), with his brothers Tom, Dick, and Jim, and his father.

A Family of Achievers

Gerald Ford wrote that his mother and father had three household rules: "Tell the truth, work hard, and come to dinner on time." The formula, though simple, worked. All the Ford boys went to college and achieved success. Tom became an optometrist; Richard was president of the Ford Paint and Varnish Company, a firm founded by his father; James served eight years in the Michigan state legislature.

☆ ☆ ☆

During high school, Jerry Ford took a part-time job at a local restaurant. "My job was to slap hamburgers on the grill, handle the cash register, and wash dishes," he recalled. One day a man stood near the restaurant's candy counter and stared at Jerry for 15 or 20 minutes without saying a word. Finally the man said, "I'm Leslie King, your father. Can I take you to lunch?"

Jerry was stunned, and he was angry. Here was a man who had made no attempt to contact him in almost 16 years. Jerry knew that a judge had ordered King to pay his mother $50 to $75 a month for child support. King had rarely made those payments even though he had considerable wealth.

At first Jerry coldly refused his father's invitation, but King persisted and Jerry finally agreed. Outside the restaurant was Leslie King's brand-new luxury car. King introduced the woman in the front seat as his wife. At lunch, King claimed that he found Jerry by going to all five high schools in Grand Rapids, asking for a boy named either Gerald Ford or Gerald King. They talked mainly about sports. Jerry found the conversation difficult and painful. At last King drove Jerry back to his restaurant, handed him $25, and said, "Now you buy yourself something, something you want that you can't afford otherwise." With a wave, Leslie King and his wife drove off and out of Jerry's life.

That night Jerry told his mother and his stepfather about the meeting. He was badly upset. He felt bitter that his biological father had burst rudely into his life after so many years of neglect. In his autobiography he wrote, "Nothing could erase the image of my real father that day: a carefree, well-to-do man who didn't really give a damn about the hopes and dreams of his first-born son." The talk with his parents was a "loving and consoling one," Ford wrote later. Even so, he continued, "When I went to bed that night, I broke down and cried."

College and Stardom ———————————————

The 1920s were good times in most of America. Jobs were plentiful. Successful businessmen were investing money in the stock market, which seemed to reach a new high each year. Then, in late 1929, the stock market crashed, and in a few months investors lost more than $40 billion. In the next few years, the market crash was followed by a severe economic depression. Factories and businesses closed, and millions of ordinary workers lost their jobs. Banks failed, wiping out the savings of hardworking families. Farmers, unable to sell their crops, lost their farms. In cities, thousands stood in long lines to get free food provided by charitable organizations.

In the fall of 1929, just weeks before the crash, Gerald Ford Sr. had bought a paint manufacturing company. Unemployed people do not buy paint to decorate their homes, and Gerald Ford's business slowed nearly to a stop. Ford had ten employees to pay and little money coming in from customers. Instead of laying off his workers, he made a deal to keep paying every employee (including himself) $5 a week, just enough to buy groceries. He promised that when business improved, everyone would get a substantial raise. When business finally got better, Ford was true to his word.

All four of the Ford sons worked at the paint company at one time or another. Workers in the factory wore coveralls. They frequently got paint on their hands and wiped their hands on the coverall legs. When Jerry worked at the factory in the summer, he preferred to wear shorts, wiping excess paint onto his bare legs. A family "Jerry joke" was that Jerry took a bath on Friday night, and then only to clean the accumulated paint off his legs.

In Jerry's last year of high school, a Grand Rapids movie theater ran a contest to choose the city's "most popular high school senior." Jerry won first prize: an all-expense trip to Washington, D.C. That trip was Ford's first visit to the nation's capital, a place where he would later make history.

Finding the money to go to college was difficult in the early 1930s as the economic depression deepened. Jerry Ford had two advantages, however. First, he was an excellent student. During his junior year of high school, his grades

GERALD FORD

NATIONAL HONOR SOCIETY; STUDENT COUNCIL; INTER-HI COUNCIL; SODALITAS LATINA; GLEE CLUB; VARSITY CLUB; FOOTBALL, CAPTAIN; FOOTBALL, SECOND TEAM; BASKETBALL, FIRST TEAM; TRACK; PHOTO COMMITTEE.

Jerry Ford in his high school yearbook.

Presidential Klutz?

Ford may have been the best athlete who ever served as president. Yet while he was in office, he once fell while coming down the steps of *Air Force One*, the presidential plane. Another time, he tripped over the feet of his own assistant. Worst of all, he hit an errant golf shot into a small crowd of spectators, hitting one of them. Replays of these stumbles became a source of humor for late-night comedians, and Ford got an undeserved reputation as a clumsy person.

☆☆☆

ranked him in the top five percent of his class. Second, Ford was one of the best high school football players in the state. As his team's center on offense, he was a rugged blocker. Like all players at the time, he also played on defense. Because of his grades and his football prowess, he won a partial scholarship to the University of Michigan. The scholarship paid his tuition, but he still worked part-time to meet his living expenses. He held various student jobs. He waited on tables in a coffee shop and cleared up dirty dishes in a hospital cafeteria.

Football was Ford's college passion. He stood about 6 feet tall (1.83 meters) and weighed about 200 pounds (91 kilograms). By today's standards he was not a big player, but in the 1930s he was big enough to achieve stardom as a lineman. Fast and quick on his feet, Jerry played center in Michigan's single wing offense. This meant he had to snap the ball through his legs to the quarterback five yards behind, then move to his left or right to block defenders. A teammate remembered Jerry as "a player who had no fear, and a smart guy too."

One of Jerry's closest college friends was a swift, pass-receiving end named Willis Ward. The future president and Ward roomed together when the team played away from home. Ward was the only African American player on the Michigan squad. In 1934, when Jerry was a senior, the team traveled south to play Georgia Tech. No college teams in the South allowed African American students or football players. Georgia Tech threatened to cancel the game with Michigan if Ward was scheduled to play. Reluctantly, Michigan officials gave in and announced that Ward would not take the field.

Ford was outraged that his good friend could not play because of his race. He considered organizing a *boycott*, in which the Michigan team would refuse to play unless Ward played with them. Ward himself talked Ford out of the boycott. "You've got to play Saturday," Ward told him. "You owe it to the team." Reluctantly Jerry Ford played. But when a Georgia Tech lineman made a racial comment about Ward's absence, Ford flattened him with a vicious block.

Ford graduated from the Michigan in 1935. His grades ranked in the top quarter of his class and he was named most valuable player on the football team. Both the Green Bay Packers and the Detroit Lions made offers to him to play pro-

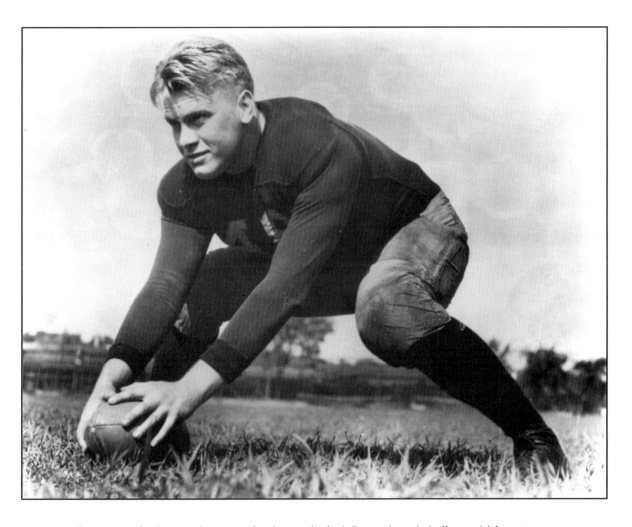

At the University of Michigan, Ford was a star of its championship football team, playing both offense and defense. He was chosen to several All-America teams.

fessional football. Pro players earned very small salaries in the 1930s, and Ford turned down the offers. He wanted to continue his education. Gerald Ford was determined to be a lawyer.

Chapter 2

Yale Law School

The Great Depression still gripped the country in 1935, when Gerald Ford graduated from college. Going to law school was a goal largely for rich young men in those hard times. Men like Ford had to look for jobs immediately after college. Ford was determined, however. Not only did he want to attend law school, he wanted to enroll at the Yale Law School in New Haven, Connecticut, one of the best in the country.

He applied for a job in Yale's athletics department and was hired as an assistant coach for the freshman football squad. In the off-season, he was to coach boxing, which he knew little about. Before leaving for New Haven, he went to the Grand Rapids YMCA to observe and to fight a few rounds against experienced boxers. He took a few hard blows, but he learned enough about the sport to become a competent coach.

Yellowstone Summer

In 1936 Ford accepted a summer job at Yellowstone National Park in Wyoming. One of his duties was to supervise "feeding time" when the bears ate scraps thrown by visitors. Tourists enjoyed the feeding sessions, but Ford stood by with a rifle in case a bear attacked an onlooker. He never had to use the rifle, although the bears fought among themselves over the food. Years later he told bedtime stories to his children about the bears in Yellowstone. Gradually he made the stories more exciting by exaggerating. Finally, the children realized he was making up the episodes. One of them said, "Dad, please don't tell me the story of the bears again."

★ ★ ★

When Ford first applied to the Yale Law School, he was turned down, so he continued his full-time coaching job. In the summer of 1937 he took some law classes at the University of Michigan. Later that year he was accepted for the term beginning in early 1938. Ford's persistence had paid off.

While traveling with the boxing team, Ford met a beautiful young woman named Phyllis Brown, a student at Connecticut College for Women. They fell in love and spoke about getting married after he finished law school. Phyllis was a blond with Hollywood-style good looks. In 1940 she was the main subject of a feature story on glamorous young people in *Look Magazine*, then a popular picture magazine. The magazine chose the handsome Gerald Ford as the male model. In this way, photos of the 26-year-old future president appeared in a national magazine. Phyllis Brown and Gerald Ford dated for more than four years. They finally agreed, however, that they were headed in different directions. Brown wanted to continue her modeling career in New York. Ford wanted to return to Grand Rapids to practice law.

In 1941, Gerald Ford received his law degree from Yale. He returned to Grand Rapids, leaving his coaching career and Phyllis Brown behind. He would soon see duty in another unexpected career.

War!

In the summer of 1941 Ford returned to Grand Rapids. Later that year, he passed the Michigan state bar examination and gained his license to practice law. He went into partnership with Philip Buchen, who would remain a friend for many years.

On Sunday, December 7, 1941, Ford was at his office catching up on his legal work. That afternoon, he learned on the radio that the Japanese had bombed the U.S. military bases in Pearl Harbor, Hawaii. In the next few days, the United States declared war on Japan, Germany, and Italy, and entered World War II.

That spring, Ford entered the navy reserves and was commissioned as a junior officer. He served as a physical fitness instructor at a base in North

Carolina. Then in 1943 he reported to the USS *Monterey*, a new aircraft carrier. His assignments were to serve as the ship's athletic director and as a gunnery officer. The *Monterey* sailed to the South Pacific, where the navy was waging war against the Japanese. The planes on the *Monterey* flew regular missions to attack Japanese bases and battle Japanese fighter planes. Time after time enemy fighter planes and bombers made screaming dives at the *Monterey*. "The Japanese planes came at us with a vengeance. We had many general quarters calls [calls to all on board to prepare for battle], and it was as much action as I'd ever hoped to see."

Ford survived the enemy aircraft, but he almost lost his life to an ancient foe of seamen—a killer storm. In December 1944, as the *Monterey* steamed near the Philippines, 100-mile-an-hour (160 kilometer-per-hour) winds lashed the ship. Waves taller than a house tossed the carrier about like a toy boat in a bathtub. The destroyer *Monaghan*, sailing near the *Monterey*, was turned upside down by a giant wave. Of its 250-man crew, 244 were drowned. On that dark rain-swept day, Ford was on deck when the ship pitched violently. "I lost my footing, fell to the deck flat on my face, and started sliding toward the port side as if I were on a toboggan slide," he recalled. He fell from the deck onto a catwalk below. Another few feet and Ford would have tumbled overboard and been swallowed up by the sea. Desperately, he held on with all his strength. It was there, clinging for his

On the USS *Monterey* during World War II, Ford helped set up the elevator floor of the huge aircraft carrier as a basketball court. Here he leaps to block a shot.

life, that Ford reflected on his mother's favorite verse from the biblical book of Proverbs: "Trust in the Lord with all thy heart; and lean not unto thine own understanding." The *Monterey* weathered the storm, but one crewman was killed and more than 30 were injured.

In early 1945, Ford was reassigned to the United States. He spent the rest of the war at Glenview Naval Air Station near Chicago, Illinois. Ford enjoyed his time in the navy. His calm leadership earned the respect of the men who served under him. A seaman named Ronald Smith remembered, "Nothing ever seemed to rattle him. One day we came under attack and I dived for cover in the hatchway. I looked up and there was Lieutenant Ford. He smiled and asked me, 'Why the hell are you in such a hurry?'"

The Lawyer and the Lady ————————————

After the war Ford returned to his law practice. He was beginning to earn a respectable income. For relaxation he played golf. He also sought out new friends and new activities. As Ford said later, "I was a compulsive 'joiner.'" He joined the American Legion, the Red Cross, and the National Association for the Advancement of Colored People (NAACP), and he worked with the Grand Rapids Boy Scouts. This volunteer spirit soon led him to his future wife.

One day in 1947, Ford had a conversation with his mother. His situation was odd. He was in his thirties, a successful lawyer, and a war veteran. Yet he was still living at home with his parents. Meanwhile, his three younger brothers were all married and raising families. His mother asked, in a tone that Ford described as "good-natured but very persistent," when he too would get married. "You're thirty-four years old," she said. "When are you going to settle down?"

Gerald Ford was dating, but he had developed no serious relationships since he broke up with Phyllis Brown. Then, while serving as a volunteer for a cancer fund-raising drive, a friend brought up the name Betty Bloomer. Ford remembered Betty as an attractive woman about his own age. He did not know her well because they had attended different high schools. The friend said that Betty was married, but had recently filed for a divorce. Ford called Betty and they met to talk.

They liked each other from the start. Betty worked as a fashion coordinator for a Grand Rapids department store. She had been a dancer in New York and had formed her own dance company in Grand Rapids. Like Ford, she was active in volunteer organizations. One of her volunteer services was giving dance classes to handicapped children. Betty later described Gerald Ford as "the most eligible bachelor (football hero, lawyer, ardent skier) in Grand Rapids." One date led to another.

Jerry and Betty Ford in 1948 soon after their wedding.

Soon Betty's divorce was final. She was free to remarry, but how could she get this shy ex-football player to pop the important question? She later wrote, "He was such a reserved man it was difficult for him even to tell me he loved me—he proposed by saying, 'I'd like to marry you.'"

The weeks leading up to the wedding were busy ones. As Betty planned the wedding, Jerry Ford conducted his first political campaign, hoping to be elected to the U.S. House of Representatives. Betty and Gerald Ford were married in Grand Rapids on October 15, 1948. A few weeks later, Ford was elected to Congress.

First Election

Gerald Ford had grown up in the Republican party. His father was a Republican, as were most of his Grand Rapids neighbors. Before the war, Ford echoed most of the traditional Republican beliefs. He believed that taxes should be kept low, that government should limit its role in people's lives, and that the nation should stay out of entanglements with foreign nations. In foreign policy, many Republicans were *isolationists*, meaning that they wanted the United States to avoid disputes and wars in the rest of the world. His wartime experience changed Gerald Ford. "I had become an ardent *internationalist*," he recalled. "Our military unpreparedness before World War II had only encouraged the Germans and the Japanese. In the future, I felt, the United States had to be strong."

In 1948 Gerald Ford announced that he would run for Congress with the support of younger reform-minded Republicans. This would be no easy race. Descendants of the conservative Dutch immigrants still held political power in Grand Rapids and the surrounding region. The congressman in Ford's district was the Republican Bartel Jonkman, an established politician from an old Dutch family. Jonkman had held the congressional seat for nearly ten years, and it seemed that no one could beat him.

In his campaign, Ford emphasized his youth and his war record. His campaign headquarters was a military-surplus shed made of corrugated sheet metal, called a Quonset hut, painted red, white, and blue. To win votes, he shook hands with factory workers as they reported to their jobs early in the morning. He visited farms in the district to chat with farmers. Sometimes he even helped the farmers pitch hay. In the primary election on September 14, 1948, Ford defeated Jonkman by almost 10,000 votes. A month later, Ford married Betty Bloomer. Then in early November, he won the general election with 61 percent of the vote and was swept into office.

During his 1946 campaign for a seat in Congress, Ford visits potential voters on a farm near Grand Rapids.

The Ford campaign headquarters in Grand Rapids was an army surplus building called a Quonset hut.

Jerry and Betty Ford had no time to settle down in Grand Rapids. Late that year they headed for Washington, D.C., where Jerry would take up his duties in January 1949. For 30 years, the Ford family would have two homes, one in Grand Rapids and the other near the nation's capital.

Chapter 3

The New Congressman

Most congressmen hire professional movers to carry filing cabinets and other equipment to their new offices. Not Ford. He never shunned physical work. Over the New Year weekend of 1949, Ford and his aide John Milanowski put on overalls and went to the House Office Building to do the moving job themselves. A guard stopped the two and refused to allow them to enter. Ford spent most of the morning convincing the guard that he was really a new congressman who simply wanted to move into his office.

Once settled into his quarters, Ford began to meet fellow congressmen. One of the first people to introduce himself said, "I'm Dick Nixon from California. I heard about your big win in Michigan, and I want to say hello and welcome you to the House." Down the hall was the office of another young member of the House of Representatives, John F. Kennedy, a Democrat from Massachusetts.

In 1949 President Harry Truman invited Ford and a few other congressmen to a private tour of the White House. On the president's desk was a famous sign: The Buck Stops Here! Truman often complained that government employees were afraid to make a decision and instead passed the responsibility to the next boss higher up. This was called "passing the buck." Truman made up the sign to indicate the buck has to stop somewhere. Ford recalled that when he saw the sign, he thought, "Well, that's a good description of a president's job."

☆ ☆ ☆

Nixon and Kennedy would later loom as important figures in Ford's life as well as in the destiny of the country.

The Fords settled in a one-bedroom apartment in the Washington neighborhood of Georgetown. Ford often walked the three miles (5 km) to the Capitol building because he needed the exercise. He tried to read every new bill he was asked to vote upon in the House. He also answered every letter he received from *constituents*, the people living in his Michigan district. As a first-term representative, he began to gain the friendship and confidence of others among the House's 435 members, especially those in his own party. He also returned regularly to Grand Rapids to keep up ties with political leaders and voters at home. In 1950 he was easily elected to his second two-year term. He would gain re-election many times in the coming years.

In the early 1950s, the Ford family moved to Alexandria, Virginia, just across the Potomac River from Washington, D.C.

The Ford family began to grow. Gerald and Betty's first child, Michael, was born in March 1950. Michael was followed by John (1952), Steven (1956), and Susan Elizabeth (1957). The Fords divided their time between a home in Grand Rapids and a home in Alexandria, Virginia, just across the Potomac River from Washington. Betty Ford lived an active life. "Our kids were into everything," she wrote, "Scouts and Little League and Sunday school. And most of their activities seemed to take place at our house. I was in the PTA. I was a den mother."

On the surface Betty Ford seemed to be a happy suburban housewife. But secretly she was beginning to develop a terrible disease. Years later she announced to the world that she was an alcoholic. She claimed that the Washington social scene made her condition worse. "In Washington," she wrote, "there is more alcohol consumed than in any other city *per capita* in the world."

Cold War Concerns

During the 1950s, the Cold War dominated political thought in America. During World War II, the United States and the Soviet Union (made up of present-day Russia and several smaller neighboring states) were allies against Nazi Germany. Soon after the war, however, their friendship cooled, as the Soviets began establishing Communist governments in countries near their borders. The two great powers became locked in the tense political and economic struggle known as the Cold War. Many Americans worried that Communists might be seeking to take over at home as well as overseas. This fear of Communism was a powerful tool for political leaders hoping to gain attention in hopes of advancing themselves to a higher office. One of those opportunistic leaders was Joseph McCarthy, a senator from Wisconsin.

In a speech in February 1950, McCarthy held a piece of paper in his hand and claimed it contained a list of "205 members of the Communist Party" who were working for the U.S. State Department. McCarthy never released those names. In fact, he was lying in order to get his name into newspaper headlines. For the next four years Senator McCarthy conducted wide-ranging investigations of Communist influence in the government, in labor unions, and in the entertainment industry. McCarthy used unfounded accusations and threats to persuade witnesses to cooperate with his investigators. He worked to ruin the reputations of those who refused. He raved, ranted, and called any opponent of his inquiries a Communist.

Political leaders were afraid of McCarthy's power. Even though many disapproved of him, they were reluctant to speak out publicly. Ford, still a junior

Senator Joseph McCarthy holds up papers he claims have evidence of Communists in the U.S. State Department. In the early 1950s, he gained wide notoriety because of his aggressive search for Communists in government, labor unions, and the movie industry.

congressman, was also reluctant. "I thought he was a professional bully and I detested him personally," he wrote later, "so I kept my distance from him. In retrospect, that was wrong. I should have taken him on. The fact that I didn't speak out against McCarthy is a real regret." Finally, in 1954, McCarthy overstepped his bounds once too often. The Senate *censured* him (officially condemned his actions), and his power was broken. He died in 1957.

In 1952 former general Dwight D. Eisenhower became the first Republican president to be elected since 1928. During his eight years in office, Republicans gained majorities in the U.S. House and Senate. Ford was a loyal supporter of Eisenhower's programs and proposals. In 1960 Eisenhower's vice president, Richard Nixon, ran for president with Ford's active support. Nixon was defeated by Democrat John F. Kennedy in a very close election. This began eight years of Democratic dominance. Once again, the Republicans were the minority party.

In 1960 Jerry Ford joins other members of Congress as part of the "GOP Truth Squad," to campaign for Republican presidential candidate Richard Nixon. (Grand Old Party, or GOP, is a nickname for the Republican party.)

Death of a President ————————————————————

November 22, 1963, dawned as a bright, clear day in Washington. Gerald and Betty Ford were driving home from a conference with their son's guidance counselor. Suddenly the program on the car radio was interrupted by a bulletin from Dallas, Texas. President Kennedy had been shot. Soon afterward, Kennedy died of his wounds.

The drama of the Kennedy assassination did not end with the president's death. Hours after he was shot, the Dallas police arrested Lee Harvey Oswald, a 24-year-old ex-Marine, and charged him with the killing. Two days later, millions watched on television while Oswald was being transferred from one Dallas jail to another. Suddenly a man in the crowd uncovered a gun and shot Oswald to death. The man was identified as Jack Ruby, the owner of a nightclub. Shocked by this chain of events, the public demanded an investigation.

A week after the assassination, Ford received a call from Lyndon B. Johnson, who had been sworn in as president soon after Kennedy's death. The president said he was appointing a commission to make an "authoritative and comprehensive investigation of the Kennedy assassination." He asked Gerald Ford to serve as one of the commission's seven members, and Ford agreed.

The chairman of the commission was Chief Justice Earl Warren, and it became known as the Warren Commission. It first met in December 1963. Over ten months, it heard testimony from 552 witnesses. Commission members traveled to Texas, where they visited the Texas School Book Depository Building and stood at the window from which the assassin, Lee Harvey Oswald, had fired at the presidential car. "Kennedy had been my friend," Ford later wrote. "The thought that we were reconstructing his assassination sent a chill down my spine."

The commission presented its final report in September 1964. The report concluded that Lee Harvey Oswald was a troubled and misguided young man who acted alone when he killed Kennedy with a long-range rifle. The commission also found no link between Oswald and his murderer, Jack Ruby.

The Warren Commission Report came under intense fire. Critics said that the commission had ignored evidence that Oswald was acting as part of a larger *conspiracy* to kill the president. Decades later, many people still believe that Kennedy was the target of a plot by the Soviet Union, by Cuba, or by haters of Kennedy in the United States. Ford disagreed. In his autobiography he wrote that the Warren Report told the truth. "I believe that the report—while not perfect—is a document of which the American people can be proud."

Republicans Rebuild

As the Warren Commission completed its work in 1964, the presidential election was approaching. President Lyndon B. Johnson was running for a full term in

After months of investigation, Chief Justice Earl Warren presents the Warren Commission Report on the assassination of President Kennedy to President Lyndon Johnson. Commission member Jerry Ford is hidden at the far left.

office. In the Republican party, young conservatives united behind Arizona senator Barry Goldwater and helped nominate him to run against Johnson. Goldwater
called for a conservative revolution to end the increasing power and size of the
federal government. He was also an outspoken anti-Communist who favored a
stronger military to defend free nations against Communist aggression.

In the November election, Johnson won 61 percent of the votes, the highest percentage in any presidential election in history. Badly defeated, Republicans began looking to rebuild their party. In the House of Representatives, a
group of Republicans known as the Young Turks decided to challenge the
Republican leader, Charles Halleck. They wanted a leader who could bring new
energy to the party leadership and help unify the Republican opposition against
a large Democratic majority. When House Republicans met to organize for the
new Congress in early 1965, the Young Turks nominated Gerald Ford of Michigan to run against Halleck. In a close election, Ford won, becoming the minority leader.

Ford's participation in the Warren Commission and his election as minority leader brought him national attention for the first time. He was featured by
newsmagazines and television news, and he became a key Republican leader.
After Goldwater's disastrous defeat, Ford helped rebuild the party. Looking

ahead, he hoped for the day when Republicans could elect a majority in the House. In that case, he would likely be chosen Speaker of the House, becoming its presiding officer and most powerful member.

Chapter 4

Troubling Times

The late 1960s and early 1970s were a bitter era in the United States. Millions of young people were questioning the authority of their parents and schools. They withdrew from their communities and experimented with dangerous drugs. Major cities were torn by destructive riots. African Americans were angry and frustrated by slow progress toward equal opportunity.

The biggest issue of all was the Vietnam War. For years the United States supported the government of South Vietnam in a war against guerrilla fighters and troops from Communist North Vietnam who wanted to unify the country under their leadership. At first, most Americans, including President Lyndon Johnson and Gerald Ford, believed that the United States had a duty to help defend South Vietnam. Others, including the protesters, argued that the Vietnamese

House minority leader Ford is honored by congressional leaders and President and Mrs. Johnson in 1967.

were fighting a civil war and that the United States had no good reason to intervene in the fighting.

By 1968 some 500,000 Americans were serving in Vietnam, yet the war continued at a deadly pace. Thousands of Americans had been killed and large parts of Vietnam were destroyed. In the United States, violent protests against the war exploded on college campuses and in major cities. Clearly Vietnam was tearing the country apart.

On January 30, 1968, Communist forces began a surprise offensive during Tet, the Vietnamese New Year holiday. They attacked more than 100 settlements and reached the outskirts of Saigon, South Vietnam's capital. American and South Vietnamese forces beat back the offensive, but it raised more doubts at home about winning the war. Demonstrations increased.

On March 30, President Johnson addressed the nation. He outlined a plan for an honorable peace in Vietnam. He described "a division in the American house," and urged Americans to support their government during troubled times. At the end of the speech, he shocked the nation by announcing he would not run for another term as president. He planned to concentrate all his efforts on bringing the war to an end.

In the next few months, the nation was rocked by more violence. Civil rights leader Martin Luther King Jr. was assassinated on April 4. Once more riots broke out in major cities. In early June, Senator Robert F. Kennedy, a brother of the slain president, was shot and killed. As an antiwar Democrat, he had just won the Democratic primary for president in California. In August during the Democratic convention in Chicago, thousands of antiwar protesters gathered outside the convention hall where violent battles broke out with police.

Republican Victories ———————————————

The turbulent events of the year put the Republican party in a strong position to win the presidency in the November election. The party had nominated Richard Nixon, who had lost the presidential election to John F. Kennedy in 1960. In 1968 Nixon promised to bring peace with honor in Vietnam and to re-establish law and order at home.

Party leaders urged Nixon to choose Gerald Ford as his vice-presidential candidate. Nixon met with Ford and invited him to join the Republican ticket. As House minority leader, Ford was among the most powerful Republicans in the country. If Nixon helped elect a Republican majority, Ford would likely be chosen Speaker of the House, realizing his greatest ambition. In contrast, vice presidents have only a few Constitutional duties and little power of their own. Ford later wrote, "I thanked Nixon for his compliment, but said I wasn't interested."

Nixon chose Spiro T. Agnew, the governor of Maryland, as his vice-presidential candidate. Ford was surprised and upset by the choice. "I couldn't believe it," he remembered. "Agnew seemed like a nice enough person, but he

Richard Nixon and Spiro Agnew wave to the Republican convention after they gained the nominations to run for president and vice president in 1968.

lacked national experience or recognition. And now . . . he was going to run for vice president. I shook my head in disbelief."

As a loyal Republican, Ford campaigned hard for the Nixon-Agnew ticket. In a close election, Nixon defeated Democrat Hubert Humphrey. Republicans gained seats in Congress, but Democrats still held majorities in the House and the Senate. On January 20, 1969, Richard Nixon was sworn in as the 37th President of the United States.

Ford continued as House minority leader. With Nixon in the White House, he had more influence, especially in planning legislative strategy. During his first term, Nixon concentrated heavily on ending the war in Vietnam.

Ford's Views on Vietnam

At first Gerald Ford supported an all-out American effort to win the war in Vietnam. He was a staunch anti-Communist, and he believed the United States was right to fight against Communist expansion. In 1967 as House minority leader, he gave a speech called "Why Are We Pulling Punches In Vietnam?" in which he urged Lyndon Johnson to send even more troops to finish the war. In the 1970s Ford began to change his mind. By then it seemed that the war might not be winnable, no matter how much was spent. "The war dragged on and on," Ford wrote in his 1979 autobiography, "and the damage it caused the United States both domestically and internationally was truly staggering." Like many other Americans, he began to think of the Vietnam War as a disastrous mistake.

☆★☆

Ford and other Republican congressional leaders meet with President Nixon in 1971.

He announced a plan to turn more of the fighting over to South Vietnamese troops and began to withdraw Americans. Meanwhile, peace talks to end the war began in Paris. By 1972 negotiations were succeeding and an agreement to end the fighting was near.

In November 1972, Nixon and Agnew ran for re-election and won a second term by a landslide. Ford was re-elected to his 13th two-year term in the House, but the House of Representatives remained solidly in Democratic hands. His hope of becoming Speaker of the House was fading, and he longed to return to private life. He decided to retire at the end of his term, after 26 years in Congress. He did not foresee that a higher calling was awaiting him.

Scandals in the White House ———————

Months before Nixon's re-election in 1972, a curious burglary took place in Washington. On the night of June 17, five men entered the Watergate (an office-apartment development) and broke into the headquarters of the Democratic National Committee. An alert security guard called police, and the burglars were arrested. The break-in raised a puzzling question: Why should anyone want to rob a political office? It turned out that the "burglars" were looking for political information and were planting "bugs" in telephones to record Democrats' phone conversations. One of the burglars was a high-ranking member of Richard Nixon's re-election committee. Eventually the Watergate incident set off the biggest political scandal in U.S. history.

Even as investigations of Watergate caught national attention, another scandal rocked the Nixon administration. In 1973 Vice President Spiro Agnew

Spiro Agnew announces that he is resigning as vice president after being charged with taking bribes and evading income taxes.

announced that he was under investigation on charges that he took bribes from Maryland contractors who wanted construction projects from the state and federal governments. At first Agnew denied the accusations, but on October 10, 1973, he resigned as vice president. He agreed not to dispute the charges against

October 10, 1973

Dear Mr. President:

As you are aware, the accusations against me cannot be resolved without a long, divisive and debilitating struggle in the Congress and in the Courts. I have concluded that, painful as it is to me and to my family, it is in the best interests of the Nation that I relinquish the Vice Presidency.

Accordingly, I have today resigned the Office of Vice President of the United States. A copy of the instrument of resignation is enclosed.

It has been a privilege to serve with you. May I express to the American people, through you, my deep gratitude for their confidence in twice electing me to be Vice President.

Sincerely,

/s/ Spiro T. Agnew

The letter Agnew sent President Nixon.

him in order to avoid a possible prison term. A federal judge later sentenced Agnew to three years of probation and fined him $10,000 for taking bribes. Agnew was the first and only vice president to resign from his office while under criminal investigation.

Vice President Ford

Through most of U.S. history, the vice presidency would have remained vacant until the next presidential election. This time, the 25th Amendment to the

Constitution, which took effect in 1967, required that a new vice president be nominated by the president and confirmed by vote in both houses of Congress. Two days after Agnew resigned, President Nixon summoned Gerald Ford to the White House. "Nixon came directly to the point," Ford later wrote. "He wanted me to be his nominee."

Ford was ready to retire from public life, and he was reluctant to expose his wife and children to the relentless publicity they would receive if he became vice president. Still, he agreed to accept Nixon's nomination. Nixon himself was suspected of wrongdoing in the Watergate scandals, and people's confidence in government was at an all-time low. Ford reasoned that his country was in trouble and that it was his duty to take the job.

For Nixon, Ford was a wise choice. Nixon knew he must nominate a political leader whose past was free of any wrongdoing. The minority leader was a faithful Republican with a long record of honest dealings. He was respected by his colleagues in Congress and by the public. Also, Ford had no connection to the scandals revealed by the Watergate break-in, which had gained national attention that summer during televised hearings by the Senate Watergate Committee.

After an exhaustive investigation of his background by the FBI, Ford was confirmed as vice president by the House of Representatives and the Senate. With sadness, he resigned his seat in the House, where he had served for 25 years. On

December 6, 1973, Gerald Ford took the oath of office and became the 40th vice president of the United States. He was the first vice president ever appointed to the office.

In his autobiography, Ford wrote, "During the three years that I expected to be vice president, I hoped to participate in major decisions." His hopes were not fulfilled. He would serve only seven months as vice president, and he had little time to participate in great decisions. Instead, he was caught up in the Watergate whirlwind that engulfed the country.

In early 1974, Vice President Ford went on a nationwide speaking tour that covered 40 states and included more than 100 speeches to defend Nixon against accusations in the Watergate scandals. Nixon continued to deny any guilt, and Ford believed him. He urged the public to support Nixon and his administration.

At the same time, however, the Judiciary Committee of the House of Representatives began an investigation to determine whether the president should be impeached—charged with "high crimes or misdemeanors" in the Watergate affair. If the full House approved impeachment charges, Nixon would be tried, with the Senate sitting as a jury. If convicted, he would be removed from office. Nixon was also contesting court orders to turn over tape recordings of his White House conversations, which might prove his guilt.

Soon after taking office as vice president, Gerald Ford addresses a meeting of newspaper editors and publishers.

Though Ford believed that Nixon had broken no laws in the Watergate affair, he still recognized unsettling traits in the president's character. Years later, he described them. "Most of us have certain hidden flaws or personality quirks that seldom come to the surface," he wrote. "In Nixon's case that flaw was pride.

. . . It was reflected in his explanations of Watergate. His pride and personal contempt for weakness had overcome his ability to tell the difference between right and wrong. What some journalists called the 'dark side' of his personality had prevailed over his judgment, which was normally sound."

As the tensions in Washington increased during the summer of 1974, Ford's position was more and more uncomfortable. As evidence of Nixon's guilt grew, it became more difficult to defend him; but it was also impossible to attack him until the rest of the story was known. Ford recalled that he felt like he was "sitting on a time bomb with a blowup likely to take place at any time."

Finally the Watergate scandal came to an climax. On July 24, 1974, the U.S. Supreme Court ordered Nixon to turn over the tapes he had so closely guarded. On July 27, the House Judiciary Committee approved three articles of impeachment against Nixon. Early in August, Nixon released a transcript of the most damaging tape. It revealed that he began plotting with his top advisers only three days after the Watergate break-in to end the FBI investigation by falsely claiming that "national security" was involved. Within hours, Nixon's public support collapsed. A delegation of leading Republicans in Congress visited him at the White House and advised him to resign. If he refused, they said, he would almost certainly be impeached and removed from office.

After resigning as president on August 9, 1974, Richard Nixon waves farewell from a helicopter on the White House lawn to his staff and supporters.

On the evening of August 8, 1974, Richard Nixon spoke to the nation. "I have never been a quitter," he declared. "To leave office before my term is completed is abhorrent to every instinct in my body. But as president I must put the interest of America first." Nixon said that a long impeachment trial would take up the all the attention of the president and the Congress and would weaken the country. "Therefore, I shall resign the presidency, effective at noon tomorrow," he continued. "Vice President Ford will be sworn in as president at that hour in this office."

The following day, Gerald Ford was sworn in as 38th President of the United States. After the ceremony, Ford told reporters, "I have not sought this enormous responsibility, but I will not shirk it."

Chapter 5

The Honeymoon Period

Like other new presidents, Gerald Ford had a brief "honeymoon period." Citizens and political leaders alike gave him a chance to demonstrate his best qualities, putting aside suspicions and resentments. Three days after he became president, Gerald Ford spoke to Congress: "Now I ask you to join with me in getting this country revved up and moving." One of Ford's first actions was to name a vice president. He nominated Nelson Rockefeller, the longtime governor of New York. Rockefeller had served in important posts in the Eisenhower administration and had been elected four times as governor of New York, serving from 1959 to 1974. He was a liberal Republican, providing a contrast to Ford's more conservative views. Although Rockefeller was opposed by some conservative Republicans, his nomination was confirmed by the Senate, and he took office on December 19, 1974.

Barely ten days after taking office as president, Ford introduces former New York governor Nelson Rockefeller, his nominee to become the next vice president. Rockefeller took office after he was confirmed by Congress.

"Rich as Rockefeller"

Nelson Rockefeller was a grandson of John D. Rockefeller, who became the richest man in the world in the late 1800s, making his money in the rapidly growing oil business. Nelson's father, John D. Rockefeller Jr., spent much of his life giving away more than $550 million of the family's fortune to worthy causes, including art museums, educational programs, and overseas development projects. Nelson devoted his career to public service, taking a special interest in diplomacy and in government reorganization. He then became the popular governor of New York, gaining election four times.

The Rockefeller family's vast fortune was so well known that their name itself suggested riches. A factory worker might hold up his Friday paycheck with a twinkle in his eye and boast, "Now I'm as rich as Rockefeller."

☆ ☆ ☆

As a start, Ford hoped to convince the nation to forgive and forget the bitterness left by the Vietnam War. On August 19, 1974, he traveled to Chicago to speak to the convention of the Veterans of Foreign Wars (VFW). Members of the VFW had been strong supporters of the war in Vietnam. Ford chose this audience to speak on a touchy subject—the young men, popularly known as "draft-dodgers," who refused to serve in Vietnam. During the war years, some 50,000 evaded the military draft. Many had fled to foreign countries, and now they were afraid to come home for fear of arrest. Ford proposed to the VFW that these young men be given lenient treatment. "I want them to come home. . . ." he said. "In my judgment, these young Americans should have a second chance to contribute their fair share of the rebuilding of peace among ourselves and with all nations." The speech was well received, but weeks later, it was overshadowed by another gesture of forgiveness.

The Nixon Pardon

On Sunday, September 8, 1974, Gerald Ford went to church. He prayed about a decision he planned to announce to the country. At 11 o'clock that Sunday morning, he addressed the nation on television: "Ladies and gentlemen, I have come to a decision which I felt I should tell you and all of my fellow American citizens as soon as I was certain in my own mind and in my own conscience that it is the right thing to do."

Ford restated his theme that it was time to put the divisive issues of the past behind and to push forward. One of those issues was the Watergate scandal. "I, as President, have the constitutional power to firmly shut and seal this book," he said. Ford then announced he was granting former President Nixon a full pardon "for all offenses against the United States which he, Richard Nixon, has committed or may have committed or taken part in" during his term as president. This broad pardon assured that the former president could never be prosecuted for any crimes he might have committed in the Watergate case or any in any other incidents uncovered by the Watergate investigators.

The Nixon pardon was greeted with shock, anger, and disgust. Many Americans believed that Nixon should be tried in a court of law for illegal actions as president, and that if convicted he should go to prison. (Several of his aides and cabinet members were convicted of crimes and served time in prison.) Others felt a sense of disappointment that the full story of Nixon's involvement in the scandals might never be told.

The White House was swamped with thousands of letters, most of them condemning Ford's action. Protesters appeared in front of the White House, shouting, "Jail Ford! Jail Ford!" The *New York Times* called the pardon, "a body blow to the president's own credibility." The *Washington Post* said the pardon was "nothing less than the continuation of a cover-up." Ford's longtime friend, Jerald F. terHorst, resigned his job as presidential press secretary because he so strongly disagreed with the Nixon pardon.

The charges that hurt Ford the most were ones attacking his honesty and character. Those accusations stemmed from his early meetings with Nixon, just

President Ford signs his pardon of Richard Nixon for any crimes the former president might have committed in the Watergate affair. The pardon was a leading news story for weeks (above) and was Ford's most controversial action as president.

after Agnew resigned. Critics claimed that Ford and Nixon had made a secret deal to spare Nixon from going to prison. A workman in Washington put it bluntly: "Oh, it was all fixed. Ford said to Nixon, 'You give me the job, I'll give you the pardon.'" After 25 years in public life, Ford's reputation as an honest and forthright officeholder was being called into question.

Ford maintained that the Nixon pardon was part of his policy to lead the nation out of the morass of Watergate. A Nixon trial would last many months and keep up the ugly spirit of conflict. Ford explained to his friend, Congressman Thomas (Tip) O'Neill, "I can't run this office of the president and have this Nixon thing running on day after day when there are so many important things to spend my time on." He also suggested that he had Nixon's well-being in mind: "Nixon is a sick man. Julie [Nixon's daughter] keeps calling me because her father is so depressed."

President Ford knew his pardon of Nixon would be controversial, but he may have underestimated the abuse he would suffer as a result. He continued to insist that there was no secret deal between him and Nixon. Watergate posed what Ford called "a self-destructive attitude which we've got to lick." He believed that the Watergate affair now belonged in the history books, not in the headlines. Still, the pardon cost Ford the trust of many Americans.

Life in the White House

On September 26, 1974, Gerald Ford got a phone call from the White House doctor. "I knew something had to be very wrong," he remembered. The doctor reported that during a routine physical exam he discovered a lump on Betty Ford's breast. The lump would have to be removed to see if it was cancerous. If the surgeons discovered cancer they must operate and remove her breast.

Ford later recalled that the night before Betty's operation "was the loneliest night of my life." The doctors did discover cancer and they operated immediately. After the operation Betty Ford suffered a brief period of mental depression. Then she cheered up and was her old smiling self. Mrs. Ford insisted that the discovery of her breast cancer and her operation be announced publicly. Women followed her case closely, and many became aware of the dangers of breast cancer for the first time. They learned that her treatment was successful mainly because the cancer was detected early. In the following months, thousands of women arranged for physical examinations for possible breast cancer. Betty Ford's openness about her condition may have saved many lives.

Betty and Gerald Ford lived a more relaxed life in the White House than many first families. Even when they entertained heads of state, they remained easygoing and informal. Perhaps the high point of their entertaining in the White House came in December 1975, when they invited 900 guests to a congressional

Betty Ford and her daughter Susan work on homemade holiday decorations in the White House. The Fords brought an informal and relaxed style to the executive mansion.

A Good Home for a Dog

The Ford family loved dogs, but their last dog, a golden retriever named Sugar, died when Ford was vice president. In 1974 White House photographer David Kennerly and the Fords' daughter Susan decided to present the Fords with a new puppy as a surprise gift. President Ford retold the story in his autobiography.

Kennerly called a man in Minnesota who bred and sold retrievers. The breeder asked the name of the dog's new owner. Kennerly said that the dog was a surprise gift and he wanted to keep the owner's name secret.

"We have to know if the dog is going to a good home," said the breeder.

Jerry Ford and the family's favorite dog, Liberty, in the Oval Office.

"The couple is friendly, and they live in a white house with a big yard and a fence around it. It's a lovely place."

"Do they own or rent?" the dog breeder asked.

David thought for a minute. "I guess you might call it public housing."

When the breeder asked if the new owner had a steady job, Kennerly gave up his secret, revealing that the dog was for the president of the United States. Soon the retriever puppy was on its way to the White House. The Fords named it Liberty.

☆ ☆ ☆

Christmas Ball. It was an evening to relax and have fun. President and Mrs. Ford were superb ballroom dancers, and they encouraged others to enjoy themselves on the dance floor.

Domestic Policies

With Watergate in the past, President Ford faced a host of new problems that were threatening the country. The first was inflation, a steady rise in the cost of every-day necessities. In 1973 the Yom Kippur War in the oil-rich Middle East had increased the cost of imported oil, raising prices for gasoline. A 1974 drought in the corn- and wheat-producing states drove up prices for groceries. When he took office, President Ford inherited what the *New York Times* called "the worst inflation in the country's peacetime history."

In the early days of his presidency, Ford established the Council on Wage and Price Stability, a group of experts to study the problems posed by inflation. Late in September 1974, he took additional steps to slow or end inflation. He personally promised to limit spending by the federal government to keep the federal deficit from increasing. Not all of his proposals were passed by the Democratic-controlled Congress, but inflation began to ease during 1975.

A second major problem was unemployment. The number of jobless workers rose to levels not seen in nearly 30 years. Ford went into action to address that problem, approving the creation of federal jobs for the unemployed. Like earlier presidents, Ford discovered that he could not always control the economy, but he addressed problems that had received little attention during the Watergate crisis.

Many of Ford's close friends were still congressmen, but his dealings with Congress as president were often difficult. He had to deal with the Democratic majority, which often opposed his programs and proposals. The Democrats passed programs of their own, many of which Ford disagreed with. In two and a half years, Ford *vetoed* 66 bills, refusing to sign them into law. Most of the bills represented parts of a Democratic plan to fight inflation. Ford and his Republican advisers believed that the plan would actually make inflation worse. Of the 66 bills he vetoed, Congress *overrode* his veto twelve times, approving these bills by two-thirds majorities in both houses. These bills became law in spite of the president's objections.

Dangers

Being president is a dangerous job. The president always travels with Secret Service agents to protect his life, but they are not always able to shield him from every hazard. In the space of a few weeks in September 1975, Ford narrowly escaped two assassination attempts.

On September 5 in Sacramento, California, a young woman in a crowd reached out as if to shake the president's hand. Suddenly Ford saw a .45-caliber pistol pointed directly at him. A Secret Service agent grabbed the woman and wrestled her to the ground before she could pull the trigger. She was Lynette "Squeaky" Fromme, a onetime follower of a notorious California murderer named Charles Manson.

On September 22, in San Francisco, California, a woman named Sara Jane Moore shot at Ford with a pistol, but missed. Both women were convicted of

President Ford (left center) begins to duck behind his limousine after a shot was fired at him on September 22, 1975. He was the target of two assassination attempts within three weeks, but was not injured in either attack.

attempted murder and sentenced to life in prison. Ford said the assassination attempts, though they were terrifying, would not affect his travel plans. "I don't think any person as president ought to cower in the face of a limited number of people who want to take the law in their own hands."

Foreign Affairs

The long Cold War between the United States and the Soviet Union continued through Gerald Ford's presidency, but there were hopeful signs of a "thaw." In 1972, Richard Nixon became the first president to visit the Soviet Union. Nixon and Soviet leaders agreed on a new policy of *détente*, an easing or relaxation of tensions. They discussed limiting their countries' huge stockpiles of nuclear weapons and increasing trade. Following this lead, Ford visited the Soviet Union in November 1974 and met with Premier Leonid Brezhnev. The two men discussed further reductions in nuclear missiles. On May 28, 1976, the United States and the Soviet Union signed an agreement to limit the size of underground nuclear explosions their scientists used when conducting weapons tests.

In foreign affairs, Ford valued the advice of Secretary of State Henry Kissinger, who promoted détente under President Nixon and worked to keep peace in other parts of the world. In 1975 Kissinger helped to settle a border dispute between Egypt and Israel. Promoting peace between Israel and its neighbors was a prime mission of the Ford administration.

In April 1975, the nation watched sadly as the final act of the long Vietnam conflict played out. American military forces had left the region a year earlier, but the U.S. government still provided aid and advice to South Vietnam. In early 1975, Northern troops pressed ever closer to Saigon, the Southern capital. On April 29, the United States helped organize an evacuation of Americans still in the country and of South Vietnamese government workers and supporters. Using small boats, planes, and helicopters, they carried about 7,100 Americans and nearly 60,000 South Vietnamese to safety on ships offshore. The South Vietnamese government collapsed, and Communist troops rushed into the city. Scenes of the last helicopters taking off from the U.S. Embassy in Saigon were televised in the United States, providing a last depressing image of the longest war the nation has ever fought. South Vietnam ceased to exist, as the Communist government of North Vietnam unified the country.

Two weeks after the fall of Saigon, Communist forces in nearby Cambodia seized an American cargo ship called the *Mayaguez*. The ship carried a crew of 39 men. Cambodia's new Communist leaders apparently wanted to heap further embarrassment on the United States after the defeat in Vietnam. The

Ford listens somberly to a report on the fall of Saigon, the capital of South Vietnam, to Communist forces in April 1975.

White House worried the *Mayaguez* crew would be held hostage. Ford acted boldly. He ordered an operation by U.S. Marines to free the men and recapture the ship. The Marines accomplished their mission, rescuing all crew members, but the cost was high—15 marines were killed and 3 were missing. In addition, 23 Air Force men were killed in the crash of a helicopter in Thailand during preparations for the assault.

Despite the grim news from Asia, President Ford visited China on December 1, 1975. As the largest Communist nation on Earth, China was another Cold

War adversary. Ford met with the 82-year-old Communist Party Chairman Mao Zedong, who had led the Communist revolution in his country. The China visit was another step in the general relaxing of tensions between the Communist and non-Communist worlds.

President Ford meets with Chairman Mao Zedong, the leader of China's Communist revolution.

When President Ford took office in 1974, he appointed former Illinois congressman Donald Rumsfeld White House chief of staff. In November 1975, he named Rumsfeld to a cabinet position as secretary of defense. Rumsfeld was the youngest man ever to serve in that post. Twenty-five years later, President George W. Bush appointed Rumsfeld to another term as defense secretary, where he took a leading role in directing military actions in Afghanistan and Iraq.

Ford in the Oval Office with his personal staff. Richard Cheney, at right, was elected vice president under George W. Bush in 2000. Donald Rumsfeld, at left, served both Ford and George W. Bush as secretary of defense.

Ford's deputy assistant in the White House, Richard Cheney, became chief of staff in 1975. Cheney later served as a congressman from Wyoming and as secretary of defense during the presidency of George H. W. Bush, from 1989 to 1993. In 2000, he was elected vice president to serve with President George W. Bush.

☆ ☆ ☆

Re-election

In July 1975, President Ford announced that he would seek election to a full term as president in 1976. This was a drastic change of mind from a man who had been planning to retire from Congress two years earlier. "I had promised Betty that I would quit politics," Ford wrote. "I fully intended to honor that pledge, but Betty released me from it. She knew how I felt about being president. She thought the country needed me, and she wanted me to run."

First Ford had to overcome a challenge from within his political party. In the fall of 1975, Ford received a phone call from Ronald Reagan, the governor of California and a leader of Republican conservatives. Reagan told the president the he would soon announce his own candidacy for president. Ford was not pleased. Reagan was challenging him for leadership of the Republican party. The battle between them was sure to cause division and bad feeling among Republicans.

To prepare for the battle against Reagan, the president's advisers warned that he must choose a new vice-presidential candidate. Vice President Rockefeller was too liberal and would make a perfect target for Reagan supporters. In November 1975, Rockefeller announced he would not run for the vice presidency.

Ford and Reagan met in a series of primary elections in the spring of 1976. Ford won a narrow victory in New Hampshire and won most other states in the Northeast and Midwest, but Governor Reagan won hundreds of delegates in the South and the West.

When the Republican convention gathered in Kansas City in August of 1976, arguments between Ford and Reagan supporters were as hot as the temperatures on the city streets. On the first ballot for the presidential nomination, Ford defeated Reagan—barely—by a vote of 1,187 to 1,070. Robert Dole, a senator from Kansas and a World War II hero, was nominated as Ford's vice-presidential running mate.

That same summer, Democrats chose Jimmy Carter, the governor of Georgia, to be their presidential nominee. Running with Carter for vice president was Walter Mondale, a senator from Minnesota. Thus the stage was set for the 1976 elections: the Republican Ford-Dole ticket against the Democratic team of Carter-Mondale.

Early in the campaign, public opinion polls showed that Jimmy Carter was running ahead of the president. Carter proved to be an attractive candidate. He was looked upon as an outsider who could bring a new spirit to Washington. Ford proposed a series of televised debates, hoping to bring his case to the public.

Jimmy Carter, the little-known governor of Georgia, gained the Democratic nomination for president in 1976. Carter defeated President Ford in November.

Neither candidate was an inspiring speaker, and the debates seemed dull to many viewers. Still, those televised exchanges helped decide the election.

In the first debate Carter looked nervous and evaded direct answers. In the second debate, Ford made a mistake. In trying to say that the countries of Eastern Europe did not accept the leadership of the Soviet Union, he said instead that the Soviet Union did not dominate Eastern Europe. Most viewers knew this was untrue, and Ford's slip of the tongue was shown over and over again on television news programs. Neither candidate was a clear winner in the debates, but Ford did not gain as much ground as he had hoped. As the election approached, polls showed that Ford and Carter were running virtually even.

On election day, only 54 percent of eligible Americans cast ballots. Because the two candidates were unexciting as personalities, many voters stayed home. When the votes were counted, Jimmy Carter won 50.1 percent of the popular vote to Ford's 48.0 percent. Carter won 297 electoral votes to Ford's 240. The results were so close that a shift of 10,000 votes from Carter to Ford in Ohio and Hawaii would have changed the result and given Ford the victory.

Why did Ford lose in 1976? Experts offer many explanations. The primary battles between Republican conservatives and moderates had divided the party, and not all Republicans supported Ford wholeheartedly. An economic slowdown in the months before the election may have cost Ford votes. Towering over all other considerations, however, was Ford's pardon of Richard Nixon. Many voters continued to believe that the pardon was an inside deal, a "fix," and they never forgave Gerald Ford.

Even Ford's critics agreed that he had served his nation well. He became the country's leader when presidential prestige and trust in government were at a low ebb. With his calm and deliberate manner, he helped restore the reputation of the presidency and move the nation past a bitter time. Toward the end of his term Ford said, "If I'm remembered, it will probably be for healing the land."

Chapter 6

A New Challenge —————————————

Gerald and Betty Ford built a retirement house in Rancho Mirage, California, near the desert community of Palm Springs. Betty had long suffered from arthritis, and her doctors hoped that the dry climate might ease her arthritis pains.

Ex-president Gerald Ford plunged into writing his autobiography, *A Time to Heal*, a plain-spoken and often amusing book. The former president also kept busy giving speeches and supporting Republican candidates in elections. However it was his wife, Betty, who attracted newspaper headlines after the president's retirement.

Betty Ford was an alcoholic. Alcoholism is a disease that strikes one in every ten Americans. Like many alcoholics, Betty Ford carried on a busy and responsible life even while suffering privately. At first, she was a social drinker, enjoying a glass of wine with dinner

Gerald and Betty Ford in retirement in 1980.

or a drink before a meal. Gradually, alcohol became a larger and larger part of her life. By the time the Fords left the White House, family members recognized the telltale signs of Betty's disease—the slurred speech, memory losses, and inability to concentrate. Betty's problem was complicated by painkilling medications doctors prescribed for her arthritis. The medications helped control her pain, but the combination of alcohol and pills became a powerful addiction that ruled her life and threatened her health.

In 1978, with the approval and the support of her family, Betty Ford announced publicly that she was an alcoholic and entered a rehabilitation hospital. Her treatment was successful. She never again took an alcoholic drink. She was quick to point out she was still a "recovering" alcoholic. The disease is never completely cured, and the rehabilitation process lasts a lifetime.

After her recovery, Betty Ford worked to help others who suffered from alcoholism. On October 3, 1982, surrounded by her friends and family, she opened the Betty Ford Center in Rancho Mirage, California. The center is a hospital and treatment center for people addicted to alcohol or other drugs. In the years since the dedication, thousands of people have received treatment at the center. In her book *Betty: A Glad Awakening*, she wrote of her feelings about the center and her role in helping others. "Sometimes I'm asked if I feel I have a

In 1999 President Bill Clinton awards the Presidential Medal of Freedom to former president Gerald Ford. Hillary Clinton applauds at left.

mission. I don't. . . . I don't think God looked down and said, 'Here's Betty, we're going to use her to sober up alcoholics. . . .' I think God has allowed me—along with thousands of others—to carry a message, a message that says, there's help out there, and you too can be a survivor."

For many years, Gerald Ford continued to speak at political gatherings, government seminars, and college graduations. He spoke at 179 different colleges and universities. In 1987 he published a second book, called *Humor and the Presidency*, which retells stories about the way presidents have used humor to amuse and persuade legislators and voters. Ford also remained an active supporter of the Boy Scouts of America and helped raise funds for the Betty Ford Center.

In August 1999, President Bill Clinton presented Ford with the Medal of Freedom, the highest award that can be given to a civilian. The citation summarizes Ford's accomplishments as president. It reads:

> Gerald R. Ford assumed the presidency and led America during a time
> of unprecedented challenge. Building on bonds of trust forged during
> 25 years of exemplary public service in the United States Congress, he
> guided our nation toward reconciliation and a reestablished confidence
> in our government. A leader of character, courage, decency, and
> integrity, he earned the nation's enduring respect and gratitude.
> America is forever indebted to Gerald R. Ford—38th President of
> the United States—for his legacy of healing and restored hope.

Fast Facts Gerald Rudolph Ford

Birth:	July 14, 1913 (name at birth: Leslie Lynch King Jr.)
Birthplace:	Omaha, Nebraska
Parents:	Leslie Lynch King and Dorothy Gardner King
	Stepfather: Gerald Rudolf Ford
Brothers:	(half brothers)
	Thomas Gardner Ford (1918–1995)
	Richard Addison Ford (1924–)
	James Francis Ford (1927–2001)
Education:	University of Michigan, graduated 1935
	Yale Law School, graduated 1941
Occupation:	Lawyer
Marriage:	To Elizabeth (Betty) Bloomer, October 15, 1948
Children:	(*see* First Lady Fast Facts at right)
Political Party:	Republican
Public Offices:	1949–1973 U.S. House of Representatives (Fifth District, Michigan)
	1963–1964 Member of the Warren Commission, which investigated the circumstances of the Kennedy assassination
	1965–1973 House Minority Leader
	1973–1974 Vice President
	1974–1977 38th President of the United States
His Vice President:	Nelson A. Rockefeller
Major Actions as President:	1974 Granted former President Nixon a full pardon for any crimes he might have committed during his presidency
	1974 Conferred with Soviet leader Leonid Brezhnev in the Soviet Union
	1975 Ordered U.S. Marines to retake the American merchant ship *Mayaguez*, seized by Cambodian forces
	1975 Visited China
	1976 Signed an agreement with the Soviet Union to limit the size of underground nuclear explosions
	1976 Proposed statehood for Puerto Rico

Fast Facts

Elizabeth Bloomer Ford (Betty)

Birth:	April 8, 1918
Birthplace:	Chicago, Illinois
Parents:	William Stephenson Bloomer and Hortense Neahr Bloomer
Brothers:	Robert
	William Jr.
Education:	Grand Rapids Central High School, graduated 1936
	Bennington School of Dance, Vermont
	Martha Graham School of Contemporary Dance, New York City
Marriages:	To William C. Warren, 1942 (divorced 1947)
	To Gerald R. Ford, in Grand Rapids, Michigan, October 15, 1948
Children:	Michael Gerald (1950–)
	John Gardner (1952–)
	Steven Meigs (1956–)
	Susan Elizabeth (1957–)
Major Issues as First Lady:	Supported efforts to promote the arts, help handicapped children, and publicize woman's issues. In retirement, she founded the Betty Ford Center, a treatment center for people with alcohol and drug dependency problems.

Timeline

1913	1914	1916	1927	1931
Leslie Lynch King Jr. (later Gerald Ford) born in Omaha, Nebraska, July 14.	Dorothy King and her son move to Grand Rapids, Michigan, December.	Dorothy King marries Gerald Rudolf Ford; her son takes name Gerald Ford.	Ford attains the rank of Eagle Scout in the Boy Scouts.	Graduates from South High School in Grand Rapids; enrolls at University of Michigan.

1945	1948	1963	1965	1968
Begins new law practice in Grand Rapids.	Marries Betty Bloomer, October; elected to Congress from Michigan's Fifth District, November; serves until 1973.	President John F. Kennedy assassinated, November; Ford appointed to Warren Commission to investigate the assassination.	Ford elected House minority leader by fellow Republicans; serves until 1973.	Republicans Richard Nixon and Spiro Agnew elected president and vice president.

1975	1976	1977	1979	1981
Visits China, meets Communist leader Mao Zedong.	Runs for election to full presidential term; defeated by Democrat Jimmy Carter.	Retires to California.	Autobiography, *A Time to Heal*, published.	Ford dedicates the Gerald R. Ford Library in Ann Arbor, Michigan.

1934	1935	1938	1941	1942

1934
Named most valuable player on Michigan football team; named to All-America teams.

1935
Graduates from University of Michigan.

1938
Begins classes at Yale University Law School.

1941
Graduates from Yale Law School, begins law practice in Grand Rapids, June; U.S. enters World War II after Japanese attack on Pearl Harbor, December.

1942
Ford joins the navy; sees combat in South Pacific on USS *Monterey*, 1943–45.

1972
Watergate break-in detected, traced to Nixon re-election committee, June; Nixon and Agnew re-elected, November.

1973
Vice President Agnew resigns, October; Ford sworn in as vice president, December.

1974
Under threat of impeachment, President Nixon resigns, Ford becomes president, August 9.

1974
Ford signs pardon of Richard Nixon, September.

1974
Visits Soviet Union to continue easing tensions of Cold War, November.

1999
Awarded the Presidential Medal of Freedom by President Clinton.

Glossary

boycott: to refuse to do something as an act of protest

censure: the action of a legislature or other official body to formally condemn the acts of a public official

conspiracy: a plot by a group of people to carry out evil or criminal acts, such as the assassination of a president

constituents: the people who live in the district of an elected official

détente: easing of tensions; in the 1970s, the word applied to easing tensions between Western nations and Communist nations through negotiation and increased trade

internationalist: in the United States, a person who believes that the country should participate in international organizations and work with other nations

isolationist: in the United States, a person who believes that the country should avoid international organizations and alliances with other governments

override: an action by Congress to pass a bill into law over a president's veto; both houses of Congress must pass the vetoed bill by a two-thirds majority

veto: a president's refusal to sign a bill passed by Congress into law

Further Reading

★ ★ ★ ★ ★

Brewster, Todd, and Peter Jennings. *The Century for Young People*. New York: Doubleday, 1999.

Joseph, Paul. *Gerald Ford*. Edina, MN: Abdo Publishing, 2000.

Kent, Deborah. *The Vietnam War*. Hillside, NJ: Enslow Publishers, 1994.

O'Shei, Tim. *Gerald Ford*. Berkeley Heights, NJ: MyReportLink.com Books, 2003.

Randolph, Sallie G. *Gerald R. Ford, President*. New York: Walker and Company, 1987.

Schulz, Randy. *Richard M. Nixon*. Berkeley Heights, NJ: MyReportLinks.com Books, 2003.

Stein, R. Conrad. *The Cold War*. Berkeley Heights, NJ: MyReportLinks.com Books, 2002.

Westerfeld, Scott. *Watergate: Turning Points in American History*. Englewood Cliffs, NJ: Silver Burdett, 1991.

MORE ADVANCED READING

Cannon, James M. *Time and Chance: Gerald Ford's Appointment with History*. Ann Arbor: University of Michigan Press, 1994.

Ford, Betty. *Betty: A Glad Awakening*. Boston: G.K. Hall, 1987.

Ford, Gerald. *A Time to Heal*. New York: Harper & Row, 1979.

Greene, John Robert. *The Presidency of Gerald R. Ford*. Lawrence: University Press of Kansas, 1995.

Places to Visit

★ ★ ★ ★ ★

The Gerald R. Ford Library
1000 Beal Ave.
Ann Arbor, MI 48109
(734) 205-0555

The library holds a vast collection of Ford's presidential papers and sponsors a variety of exhibits, presentations, and discussions.

The Gerald Ford Museum
303 Pearl St. NW
Grand Rapids, MI 49504
(616) 254-0400

Permanent exhibits on the life and times of Gerald Ford, concentrating on his years as president.

Gerald Ford Birthplace Park
3202 Woolworth Ave.
Omaha, NE 68105

This city park has been built on the site of the house where Ford was born in 1913.

The White House
1600 Pennsylvania Avenue NW
Washington, DC 20500
24-hour Visitors' Info: (202) 456-7041

Gerald and Betty Ford lived here from 1974 until early 1977.

Online Sites of Interest

★ **Internet Public Library, Presidents of the United States (IPL POTUS)**

http://www.potus.com/grford.html

Includes concise information about Ford and his presidency and provides links to other sites of interest.

★ **American President.org**

www.americanpresident.org/history/

Offers information about American presidents and the presidency, and includes a biography of Gerald Ford.

★ **Grolier**

http://gi.grolier.com/presidents/

This site, sponsored by the publisher of reference material, offers links leading to information about all the presidents. Material includes brief biographies at different reading levels, presidential portraits, and presidential election results.

★ **The White House**

www.whitehouse.gov/history/presidents

Offers brief biographical articles on each president and first lady.

★ **The Gerald R. Ford Museum**

http://www.fordlibrarymuseum.gov/

Provides biographical and other information about Gerald Ford, his family, and his presidency. It also gives additional information about the library in Ann Arbor, Michigan; and the museum in Grand Rapids.

Table of Presidents

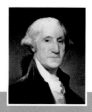 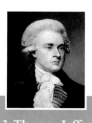 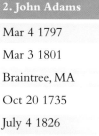 

	1. George Washington	2. John Adams	3. Thomas Jefferson	4. James Madison
Took office	Apr 30 1789	Mar 4 1797	Mar 4 1801	Mar 4 1809
Left office	Mar 3 1797	Mar 3 1801	Mar 3 1809	Mar 3 1817
Birthplace	Westmoreland Co, VA	Braintree, MA	Shadwell, VA	Port Conway, VA
Birth date	Feb 22 1732	Oct 20 1735	Apr 13 1743	Mar 16 1751
Death date	Dec 14 1799	July 4 1826	July 4 1826	June 28 1836

	9. William H. Harrison	10. John Tyler	11. James K. Polk	12. Zachary Taylor
Took office	Mar 4 1841	Apr 6 1841	Mar 4 1845	Mar 5 1849
Left office	Apr 4 1841•	Mar 3 1845	Mar 3 1849	July 9 1850•
Birthplace	Berkeley, VA	Greenway, VA	Mecklenburg Co, NC	Barboursville, VA
Birth date	Feb 9 1773	Mar 29 1790	Nov 2 1795	Nov 24 1784
Death date	Apr 4 1841	Jan 18 1862	June 15 1849	July 9 1850

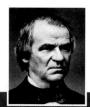   

	17. Andrew Johnson	18. Ulysses S. Grant	19. Rutherford B. Hayes	20. James A. Garfield
Took office	Apr 15 1865	Mar 4 1869	Mar 5 1877	Mar 4 1881
Left office	Mar 3 1869	Mar 3 1877	Mar 3 1881	Sept 19 1881•
Birthplace	Raleigh, NC	Point Pleasant, OH	Delaware, OH	Orange, OH
Birth date	Dec 29 1808	Apr 27 1822	Oct 4 1822	Nov 19 1831
Death date	July 31 1875	July 23 1885	Jan 17 1893	Sept 19 1881

  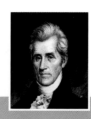 

5. James Monroe	6. John Quincy Adams	7. Andrew Jackson	8. Martin Van Buren
Mar 4 1817	Mar 4 1825	Mar 4 1829	Mar 4 1837
Mar 3 1825	Mar 3 1829	Mar 3 1837	Mar 3 1841
Westmoreland Co, VA	Braintree, MA	The Waxhaws, SC	Kinderhook, NY
Apr 28 1758	July 11 1767	Mar 15 1767	Dec 5 1782
July 4 1831	Feb 23 1848	June 8 1845	July 24 1862

13. Millard Fillmore	14. Franklin Pierce	15. James Buchanan	16. Abraham Lincoln
July 9 1850	Mar 4 1853	Mar 4 1857	Mar 4 1861
Mar 3 1853	Mar 3 1857	Mar 3 1861	**Apr 15 1865•**
Locke Township, NY	Hillsborough, NH	Cove Gap, PA	Hardin Co, KY
Jan 7 1800	Nov 23 1804	Apr 23 1791	Feb 12 1809
Mar 8 1874	Oct 8 1869	June 1 1868	Apr 15 1865

21. Chester A. Arthur	22. Grover Cleveland	23. Benjamin Harrison	24. Grover Cleveland
Sept 19 1881	Mar 4 1885	Mar 4 1889	Mar 4 1893
Mar 3 1885	Mar 3 1889	Mar 3 1893	Mar 3 1897
Fairfield, VT	Caldwell, NJ	North Bend, OH	Caldwell, NJ
Oct 5 1829	Mar 18 1837	Aug 20 1833	Mar 18 1837
Nov 18 1886	June 24 1908	Mar 13 1901	June 24 1908

	25. William McKinley	26. Theodore Roosevelt	27. William H. Taft	28. Woodrow Wilson
Took office	Mar 4 1897	Sept 14 1901	Mar 4 1909	Mar 4 1913
Left office	**Sept 14 1901•**	Mar 3 1909	Mar 3 1913	Mar 3 1921
Birthplace	Niles, OH	New York, NY	Cincinnati, OH	Staunton, VA
Birth date	Jan 29 1843	Oct 27 1858	Sept 15 1857	Dec 28 1856
Death date	Sept 14 1901	Jan 6 1919	Mar 8 1930	Feb 3 1924

	33. Harry S. Truman	34. Dwight D. Eisenhower	35. John F. Kennedy	36. Lyndon B. Johnson
Took office	Apr 12 1945	Jan 20 1953	Jan 20 1961	Nov 22 1963
Left office	Jan 20 1953	Jan 20 1961	**Nov 22 1963•**	Jan 20 1969
Birthplace	Lamar, MO	Denison, TX	Brookline, MA	Johnson City, TX
Birth date	May 8 1884	Oct 14 1890	May 29 1917	Aug 27 1908
Death date	Dec 26 1972	Mar 28 1969	Nov 22 1963	Jan 22 1973

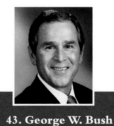

	41. George Bush	42. Bill Clinton	43. George W. Bush	
Took office	Jan 20 1989	Jan 20 1993	Jan 20 2001	
Left office	Jan 20 1993	Jan 20 2001	—	
Birthplace	Milton, MA	Hope, AR	New Haven, CT	
Birth date	June 12 1924	Aug 19 1946	July 6 1946	
Death date	—	—	—	

29. Warren G. Harding	**30. Calvin Coolidge**	**31. Herbert Hoover**	**32. Franklin D. Roosevelt**
Mar 4 1921	Aug 2 1923	Mar 4 1929	Mar 4 1933
Aug 2 1923•	Mar 3 1929	Mar 3 1933	**Apr 12 1945•**
Blooming Grove, OH	Plymouth, VT	West Branch, IA	Hyde Park, NY
Nov 21 1865	July 4 1872	Aug 10 1874	Jan 30 1882
Aug 2 1923	Jan 5 1933	Oct 20 1964	Apr 12 1945

37. Richard M. Nixon	**38. Gerald R. Ford**	**39. Jimmy Carter**	**40. Ronald Reagan**
Jan 20 1969	Aug 9 1974	Jan 20 1977	Jan 20 1981
Aug 9 1974★	Jan 20 1977	Jan 20 1981	Jan 20 1989
Yorba Linda, CA	Omaha, NE	Plains, GA	Tampico, IL
Jan 9 1913	July 14 1913	Oct 1 1924	Feb 6 1911
Apr 22 1994	—	—	June 5 2004

• Indicates the president died while in office.

★ Richard Nixon resigned before his term expired.

Index

★ ★ ★ ★ ★

About the Author

R. Conrad Stein was born in Chicago. At age 18 he joined the Marine Corps and served three years. He later attended the University of Illinois, from which he graduated with a degree in history. Mr. Stein is a full-time writer of books for young readers. Over the years he has published more than 100 books, most of them histories and biographies. Mr. Stein lives in Chicago with his wife Deborah Kent (also an author of books for young readers) and their daughter, Janna.